The Century of Networking

CIS Occasional Papers 51

The Century of Networking

Rupert Murdoch

THE ELEVENTH ANNUAL JOHN BONYTHON LECTURE

The Grand Hyatt
Melbourne

20th October 1994

THE CENTRE FOR
INDEPENDENT
STUDIES
1994

Published November 1994 by

The Centre for Independent Studies Limited

National Library of Australia

Cataloguing–in–Publication Data:

Murdoch, Rupert, 1931- .
The century of networking.

ISBN 1 86432 003 6.

1. Mass media and technology. 2. Mass media and technology - Australia. 3. Mass media - Economic aspects. 4. Mass media - Social aspects. 5. Information networks. I. Centre for Independent Studies (Australia). II. Title. (Series: CIS occasional papers; 51. (Series: John Bonython lectures; 11th).

302.23

Printed by Lindsay Yates & Partners, Artarmon NSW.
Typeset in Garamond 10pt.

Opening Remarks

Maurice L. Newman
Chairman, CIS Executive Board

Distinguished guests, ladies and gentlemen. On behalf of the Centre for Independent Studies it is my very special pleasure to welcome you all to this Eleventh John Bonython Lecture. I think you will agree this is quite an occasion. It certainly speaks volumes for our speaker that we have in this room some 850 people and we turned several hundred others away.

I would also like to say that it is a very special pleasure to have with us this evening Dame Elisabeth Murdoch and Mrs Shirley Bonython. Dame Elisabeth certainly needs no introduction to anybody here, and after all it is because of her that we have our speaker. Mrs Shirley Bonython, wife of the late John Bonython is also a very special guest to us, as is the family, the Bonython family, because it carries on the association which was built up by John Bonython who was our founding Chairman of Trustees and who did so much to get the Centre for Independent Studies underway. Greg Lindsay, of course, in his famous garage in 1976 founded the CIS, but it was John Bonython's persistence and the generosity and encouragement of the Melbourne business community which did much to get the Centre established. It is a special pleasure also to see so many of the people who were there at that original time, people like Rod Carnegie, John Macleod, Bruce Kirkpatrick, Ross Parish, Mike Porter, and so on, here tonight.

My purpose is to make just a few introductory remarks. The John Bonython Lecture was established in 1984, and named as I said for John Bonython, the first Chairman of the Centre's Board of Trustees. Over the path of eleven years it has been presented by an extraordinary range of speakers including Nobel laureate, James Buchanan; the Czech Prime Minister, Václav Klaus; and the Peruvian novelist, Mario Vargas Llosa.

The purpose of the John Bonython Lecture is 'To examine the relationship between individuals and the economic, social and political factors that make up a free society.' In association with the lecture, the Centre has established the John Bonython Lecture and Scholarship Fund, which besides supporting the Lecture's presentation and publication, makes available scholarships for young people to attend important conferences and seminars. The Fund is serving a very useful purpose and certainly is worthy of support.

We are extremely privileged that Rupert Murdoch has accepted our invitation to present the 1994 Lecture. Thank you all for joining us and I wish you a pleasant dinner and please enjoy this informal part of the evening.

Introduction

Alan McGregor
Chairman, CIS Board of Trustees

Good evening ladies and gentlemen. Tonight we will be hearing from one of the world's great entrepreneurs and business leaders. He follows a remarkable array of world figures who have presented this lecture in the past. We like to think it is the premier event of its type in Australia. But before this excitement, someone's got to give the commercial, so I'd like to say a little about the Centre for Independent Studies.

It's now a little over eighteen years since Greg Lindsay, the Executive Director and founder of the Centre, began to implement his entrepreneurial vision of an organisation which would make a difference to the way Australians face and think about the great issues that affect them. From the backyard shed that you've heard about to this gathering is quite a leap. During that time, the output from the Centre, has been demonstrably important to public debate in Australia and New Zealand. The Centre's range of activities is really quite extraordinary for a small organisation. In the last year alone it has published about a dozen books and monographs, four issues of its journal *Policy*, and six issues of a newsletter for economics teachers called *The Economics Education Review.* It has held around a dozen seminars and conferences for public participation, a further eight for high school teachers, and much more. If press coverage means anything, and who in tonight's gathering would say it doesn't, its files over the last year are inches thick. It really is, to use Paul Kelly, the Editor of *The Australian's* words, 'A think tank of world class making a sustained contribution to policy debate.'

From the beginning, the Centre has been a pioneer in producing well researched, informative and, we hope, influential work on leading policy issues – whether it be privatisation, deregulation of financial markets, tariff policy, encouraging entrepreneurship, or reforming our health care system, to name a few. There's no shortage of opportunities or problems, both social and economic, that will continue to need that combination of expert analysis and independence that is the hallmark of the Centre. In addition to its work in economic policy, constitutional reform and the like, a special effort is now being made to integrate economic analysis with some of the pressing social issues that confront us – particularly as they affect children and young adults. These issues include family breakdown, the welfare system and the disincentives that seem to be part of it, youth unemployment, and deteriorating standards in school education. No matter how extensive the nation's investment in physical capital, it will not contribute as effectively if the social fabric continues to fray.

The Centre is undertaking a major program called 'Taking Children Seriously', to bring forward policy ideas and options, to deliver social welfare programs more effectively, and to seek ways to reduce lifetime expectations of dependence and lack of incentive. If we do not improve in this area as a nation, the costs will be overwhelming. And who will pay? Business is sure to be a major contributor, and that affects most people in this room.

I would ask everybody here to reflect on the vulnerability of our liberties and our good fortune, and not to take them for granted. And never to take for granted that there will always be independent bodies like the Centre to take the lead in developing and articulating the ideas that are the basis of good public policy. Places like this survive because there are people who value a free society and free markets, and those who give financial support to help us constantly reinforce these ideals.

The world of business cannot afford to ignore the kind of society and the kind of economy that will allow it to prosper. It is not putting it too strongly to say that the CIS is performing the role of a strategic thinker for enterprise and the wider community. It is doing a job that is vital but which very few businesses connect with their bottom line and their short term outlook. What the CIS stands for could well be crucial to these aspects in years to come. It is ironic that many businesses put considerable resources into product research and development and yet perhaps miss the relevance of the kind of social and economic environment conducive to profitable market conditions.

I suspect there are many here who are not familiar with the work of the Centre. We would, of course, like everybody to become familiar and feel that making a contribution to supporting the work was worthwhile. As I do, I am sure that anyone who has subscribed will get great value from an association with what I believe is a very creative and forward-looking organisation.

Now for the more pleasant part of my task, and that is to introduce Rupert Murdoch – which is a bit silly because everybody knows him extremely well. To be parochial I could say that plenty of good things come from Adelaide. John Bonython lived there and Rupert Murdoch started his business career there with the evening newspaper called *The News* in 1954. Ironically John Bonython was Chairman of *The Advertiser* which at the time was his major competitor, but which is now part of the News Limited organisation. From Adelaide, Rupert Murdoch has moved to be the principal proprietor and chief executive of the world's most powerful and forward-looking media organisation, with involvement in newspapers, television of all types and other publishing interests. The information revolution is upon us and Mr Murdoch, as the title of tonight's lecture indicates, will undoubtedly be playing a significant role in the coming development of networking. The impact of the information explosion on the individual and his or her relationship with the state is the very type of issue that caused the establishment of this lecture series. The end of socialism as an intellectual force and the discrediting of central planning is as much a result of more information in the hands of individuals as anything else. Rupert Murdoch's company is undoubtedly one of the world's most successful over the past forty years and many investors have also benefited from his management and vision – not to mention the employment and general economic activity he has generated. All of us associated with the CIS are extremely grateful to you, Sir, for supporting this organisation and agreeing to give tonight's lecture.

I now have the greatest pleasure in inviting you, Sir, to deliver the John Bonython Lecture for 1994.

About the Author

Rupert Murdoch was born in Melbourne in March 1931. He graduated from Oxford University in 1953 and after working at the *Daily Express* in London, returned to Australia.

In 1954 he took control of News Limited. In 1968 News Limited expanded into the United Kingdom. In the 1980s the company came to own newspapers in all Australian states, established extensive media interests in the United States, and purchased Times Newspapers and the publisher HarperCollins. Through the acquisition in 1993 of a majority stake in satellite broadcaster, STAR Television, News now reaches 45 million people in 38 countries across Asia. It will soon be providing more than 20 channels of movies, sports, news and entertainment programs to European viewers, through British Sky Broadcasting.

Mr Murdoch is currently Chairman and Chief Executive of The News Corporation Limited. In 1984, Mr Murdoch was awarded the Companion of the Order of Australia (AC) for services to the media and to newspaper publishing in particular.

The Century of Networking

Rupert Murdoch

Let me start by saying what a great pleasure it is for me to be here tonight in Melbourne, the city of my birth. And so close once again to so many of the institutions that formed me – such as Toorak Presbyterian Church, where my grandfather occasionally preached, Geelong Grammar School – and even the Flemington Racecourse.

It is also a pleasure, and a privilege, to be giving this year's John Bonython Lecture for the Centre for Independent Studies. Of course, I knew both John Bonython, and the distinguished Adelaide family from which he came, very well. I believe I may even have had a tiny hand in his introduction to the oil and gas business, where he made such a contribution to South Australia. Furthermore our families had a long and entertaining relationship through Advertiser Newspapers which, when I first became publisher of the Adelaide *News* in 1953, showed its commitment to competitive enterprise by making a determined effort to run me out of town! Eventually we declared an honourable draw. I am happy tonight to pay particular tribute to John Bonython's memory.

The Centre for Independent Studies, of course, is one of the remarkable universe of similar think-tanks around the world. All are inspired with the principles of classical liberalism that are fundamental to our civilisation. Each one is now following its own independent course, but all can be traced back to a founding 'big bang', the celebrated Institute for Economic Affairs in London, which was such a powerful influence on the government of Margaret Thatcher.

And I note with great interest, incidentally, that the secret of all these institutes' success seems to be that they each find strong individuals to lead them. This is very much in accordance with my own discovery that newspapers and media companies, which like think-tanks are basically in the ideas business, cannot be run by committee.

The Centre for Independent Studies has been fortunate indeed in Greg Lindsay. I believe its recent program called 'Taking Children Seriously', focusing on the impact of government policy upon the family and upon the child, is an important example of how abstract economic theory can be translated into the most urgent terms of flesh and blood.

I said a moment ago that the Centre has a sort of celestial relationship with the Institute for Economic Affairs and, of course, above the door of its London offices, the IEA has the famous lines with which John Maynard Keynes finished his *General Theory*. They go, and I quote:

> The ideas of economists and political philosophers, both when they are right and when they are wrong, are more powerful than is commonly understood. Indeed, the world is ruled by little else. Practical men, who believe themselves to be quite exempt from any intellectual influences, are usually the slaves of some defunct economist. Madmen in authority, who hear voices in the air, are distilling their frenzy from some academic scribbler of a few years back. I am sure that the power of vested interests is vastly exaggerated compared with the power of ideas.

Now, of course and contrary to some rumours, I am not 'a madman in authority' – so I suppose I have to admit to being one of those 'practical men'. It is clearly true, however, that in the media business we are all ruled by ideas.

In the immediate sense, these are technological. Those of us who make our living by putting news and ideas and their audiences together face changes, triggered by science, that are no longer differences of degree: they amount to differences of kind. This is not so with all businesses. For example, in John Bonython's oil and gas business, if I may say so, the issue, stripped to its essentials, is still that the oil is down there in the ground and you've got to get it up and out – faster, cheaper, more efficiently, no doubt – but still, up and out. By contrast, in the news business, because people keep on inventing things, it is not even clear who will be doing the editing in the future – whether the audience will accept a package of news or whether they will want programmed gadgets to select for themselves among all available news items, something that will be entirely feasible technically – let alone whether the system that delivers the news will be hard copy or electronic; and if electronic, whether by satellite, cable or cassette.

The news business is running on a sort of metaphysical rolling log. It is what keeps us young. Or at least fit.

However, there is a more general sense in which we in the media business are influenced by ideas. I don't believe that you can contemplate the process of change in our business, and the wider effects that those changes have had upon society and upon the world, without being driven to broader conclusions about human affairs. Which is why, in the end, I am here tonight – and which is something I'll return to later.

Let me begin with a story. Almost exactly a hundred years ago, in May 1896, a young man, he was only just 30, sat in a London office awaiting the results of his latest publishing venture: the launch of a new popular daily newspaper, *The Daily Mail*. His name was Alfred Harmsworth. Later he was to become Lord Northcliffe – and later still, incidentally, he played a key role in the fortunes of my own family.

According to legend, the future Lord Northcliffe had told his associates that launching *The Daily Mail* was a gamble that meant 'bankruptcy or Berkeley Square'. And he had been in the office two straight days and two nights, getting the paper to press.

Finally, the sales reports came in. Northcliffe had gone on the record as hoping that *The Daily Mail* could sell 100,000 copies, but on that first day, it sold nearly 400,000. And it was well on its way to becoming the first English-language newspaper to reach the then miraculous mark of a million copies a day. Northcliffe responded to this with the poetry and high-mindedness we have come to expect from media moguls. Turning to his chief lieutenant, he said 'We've struck a goldmine!' I might note that this sort of instant success is very rare in publishing. Usually, you have to stick with a publication for a long time until it finds its readers. It took twenty years before we made a profit on *The Australian*. Which I guess is another reason you can't have media companies run by investment managers.

Northcliffe's launch of *The Daily Mail* was one of those magic moments that are both symptomatic and symbolic. He was the nexus, the nodal point on a network of profound forces that were developing in late nineteenth century society.

What suddenly came together that day in May 1896, was – firstly, that Britain's rail system had created a national market; secondly, radical advances in printing and paper technology making it possible to generate enormous press runs; and, thirdly, a previously unsuspected mass audience, newly literate because of the educational reforms of the 1870s and 1880s.

Print abruptly ceased to be only an elite medium and became also a popular medium. (*The Daily Mail* was priced at a halfpenny when all other papers were priced at a penny – and price matters in all markets, as we are showing in London today.) Eventually, this happened all over the world. But it was because of Northcliffe's very real genius for popular journalism that it happened in Britain so dramatically and decisively.

And part of Northcliffe's genius, if I may say so, is that he had an eye for talent. That was how he later came to know my father, a young Australian journalist who arrived in London in 1915 with a graphic story about the disaster at Gallipoli, where Northcliffe's own nephew had just been killed.

When my father came back home to Melbourne to be the editor of *The Herald*, he remembered Northcliffe's lessons and kept in touch with him. And when Northcliffe came out to Australia in 1921, he visited my father here in Melbourne. At my father's request, on the ship back home, Northcliffe read back issues of the Melbourne *Herald* and dictated comments on them, which I still have.

In vital ways, his comments are still intensely relevant to the media business today. For example, Northcliffe stressed the importance of news, and lots of it. That's something we still emphasise in all our newspapers, at a time when many newspapers are giving up the struggle with television and turning themselves into daily lifestyle magazines.

Even our much-maligned London tabloid, *The Sun*, which is in a ferocious competition with other popular papers, always has more, longer and better written stories than any television newscast. And it gets those stories read by about a quarter of the adult population of Britain.

Northcliffe also vehemently denounced what he saw as the tendency of advertisements to dominate *The Herald's* pages. This was a battle he fought in his own papers throughout his career. I mention it just to show that the free market works in subtle and self-correcting ways. The capitalist press is not a slave to advertisers: in the interest of its own survival it can only have a limited and uneasy alliance with them.

Now, I don't want to make too much of the Murdoch family's connection to Northcliffe – because, apart from anything else, he did eventually go mad! But it is an interesting thought that the whole brilliant episode of the rise of the mass media is in the careers of so few men.

And I think there's no doubt that the type of mass popular journalism that Northcliffe brought to newspapers has now extended to television. That's why News Corporation has got involved with Sky Television in Britain, Fox Television in America, STAR Television in Asia, and Vox in Germany. It's why we have 24 hour

TV news in Britain.

I hope you won't get me wrong. I have always said that personally I prefer newspapers to television. And I believe newspapers, and mass circulation newspapers, will be here, and very profitably here, for a long time to come. But the growth is going to be in television – and other, even more exotic, electronic media.

When you think about it, those years around the turn of the century, when Northcliffe was rising to the peak of his career and my father was just beginning his, were an amazing period. At that time also, technological change – the telephone, the motor car, the aeroplane – was so radical as to amount to a difference in kind, rather than degree, in the way that people have lived for centuries, indeed millennia.

Now again today, equally profound forces are at work in the world. Right now, anyone anywhere in the world is able to go to a computer screen, exchange messages with anyone anywhere else in the world, get information, news and entertainment, work and play, at minimal cost – and at no marginal cost for distance.

What this means, at the very least, is that whole new audiences and markets are being created. In the near future there are going to be many more magic moments when the new Northcliffes suddenly find that they have struck new goldmines. I don't know, no one knows, precisely what these new goldmines will be. But we are all doing our best to find out!

I do know, however, that this new era of technological change has revolutionised Australia's position in the world. Australia's first two centuries, as I said three years ago when I spoke at the University of Melbourne, were the centuries of rent-capturing – capturing what economists call 'rents', profits from primary products sold into the world market. The returns from these products had to be exceptional, because they had to overcome what Geoffrey Blainey has called, in a well-known phrase, the tyranny of distance. In fact, as you are all aware, it was the Australian gold rush in the middle of the nineteenth century that provided the first boost to this great city of Melbourne. (I'm talking about old-fashioned boring real gold here! – not the infinite gold of the mind and the market.)

But the next century will be one in which the tyranny of distance has been abolished. For Australia, it will be the century of networking. Australia will profit from its strategic location, as a highly-educated, English-speaking society that because of technological change is now as integrated in the world economy as any place on earth. Melbourne-

Manchester-Manhattan-the middle of the MacDonnell Ranges – it's all going to be the same. New Northcliffes will strike unsuspected global goldmines while physically located right here in Australia, perhaps publishing software or some specialised information product for sale on an international electronic network.

They won't ever have to go to London and be called rude names for saving the British newspaper industry!

Assuming, that is, that government policy allows Australian entrepreneurs easy access to imported computer hardware – on which to develop what will really count: the software. And assuming that it does not tax them to the point where they decide to take their goldmines, all nice and portable in a laptop's hard disk, and go off elsewhere.

All this sounds very optimistic – and it is. We have it within our power to make Australia an economic powerhouse in one of the brightest eras of human history.

So why are we so surprised? I think one of the reasons is a congerie of attitudes epitomised by George Orwell's great futuristic novel *Nineteen Eighty-Four*. Briefly, Orwell thought that technology would lead to tyranny. He thought that it would enormously enhance the power of the centralised totalitarian state, which would literally be able to keep an eye on its citizens through two-way television screens installed in their homes. He summed it up with one of a number of Orwellian phrases that have entered the language: 'Big Brother is watching you.'

I was at Geelong Grammar in 1949 when *Nineteen Eighty-Four* was published. I have to admit that I don't remember anything about the stir it caused – although I can remember the winner of the Melbourne Cup that year! It was Foxzami.

But I did arrive in England in 1950 to go to Oxford. And I vividly recall the rationing, the queues, the shortages, the shabbiness, the general weariness, that made only too credible the soul-destroying privations of the future total-welfare state that Orwell envisaged.

Now, George Orwell was a writer of genius and *Nineteen Eighty-Four* is a work of inspiration. In recent years, for example, it has become a great favourite in the former Iron Curtain countries because of its uncanny insight into the psychology of corrupt totalitarian bureaucracies. Orwell, of course, had no direct experience of this. But he was apparently able to figure it out intuitively – based on his wartime stint working for the BBC. I don't know whether it would have been different if he had been working for the ABC!

Nevertheless, the plain fact is that Orwell was wrong in his central prediction. Technology has not led to centralisation and tyranny – rather the reverse.

I've been musing about this recently because I've been reading the galleys of a very impressive new book on exactly this theme, by Peter Huber, an American lawyer and scientist – and, indeed, a fellow of another think-tank in the same constellation as the CIS: the Manhattan Institute in New York. It's an essay on why Orwell went wrong, combined with a rewriting of *Nineteen Eighty-Four* to illustrate what might actually have happened.

Huber rewrote *Nineteen Eighty-Four* by a particularly ingenious method: he scanned Orwell's collected works into his computer, and then picked up and chose and reorganised pieces of Orwell's prose. I think this is the closest that anyone has yet come to fulfilling the long-standing dream of all editors: to be able to put newspapers together without having to deal with journalists!

Huber's book is being published by Simon & Schuster in New York – regrettably one of our competitors. It's called *Orwell's Revenge: The 1984 Palimpsest*.

What is a 'palimpsest'? I had to look it up too. It's a writing surface, like a tablet or parchment, that can be scraped clean and written on again. Orwell used the word to describe history in his nightmare world – constantly rewritten, with newspaper files and reference books retrospectively altered, to suit the ruling party's current line. And, indeed, this was exactly what Stalin was beginning to do in the Soviet Union. We've even seen an odd attempt or two around here recently!

The destruction of the collective memory – something Alexander Solzhenitsyn defined in his 1970 Nobel Prize speech as the essence of totalitarianism – was a spectre that haunted Orwell. He had written with horrified fascination, in a 1944 essay, of the Caliph Omar's destruction of the libraries of Alexandria. Burning manuscripts kept the public baths warm for eighteen days. Great numbers of tragedies by Euripides and others were lost forever, including great works by Aristotle, Plato and others.

Right away, we can see the difference that technology has made. The Xerox machine – which of course did not exist even in Orwell's day – has made keeping track of original documents, so they can be rounded up and destroyed, an impossible dream. Xerox machines have also made the copying of subversive or sensitive documents for publication or leaking quite unstoppable. Which is why Xerox machines in the Soviet Union were kept under lock and key as late as the mid-1980s.

But we should also note the next step: the collective memory will hardly have a physical existence at all. It will escape into cyberspace, transmitted back and forth by modem and even satellite between scores of millions of computer network users. Solzhenitsyn took the title of his Nobel Prize speech from the Russian proverb: 'One word of truth outweighs the whole world.' In the future, we will have many words of truth, ever-present in the ether.

Why was Orwell wrong? Peter Huber argues that it was for two basic reasons. Firstly, Orwell was wrong to suppose, in the words of one of the slogans of his totalitarian party in *Nineteen Eighty-Four* that 'ignorance is strength'. In a system based on science, ignorance is not strength: it is weakness.

In Huber's scenario, a situation arises in which the party is simply unable to maintain its two-way telescreens because of a shortage of technical personnel. The screens are co-opted by enterprising 'proles' – the proles you will remember, are the underclass outside the party circle – who exploit the screens' interactivity to communicate with each other. Far from being a centralising device, the telescreen network decentralises and diffuses power.

What makes Huber's scenario the more convincing is that this sort of scientific and technological atrophy was exactly what destroyed the Soviet Union. Without freedom of inquiry, scientific inquiry just could not proceed.

By the mid-1980s, there were extraordinary reports of Western scientists going to the Soviet Union on some joint venture, finding that two separate groups of Soviet scientists were working on the same problem in ignorance of each other, sometimes even in the same city, and putting them in touch with each other. Science was being strangled by the security needs of the Soviet state. When President Reagan launched his Star Wars program, it was the last straw. The Soviets knew they could never match it and their will broke.

The second reason that Orwell was wrong, Huber argues, is in effect contained in another of his totalitarian party's slogans: 'Freedom is slavery.' But freedom is not slavery. Specifically, free markets are not monopolies.

Orwell believed that free markets must lead to private monopoly and hence to the driving-down of living standards. He believed this because, like a lot of intellectuals who are accustomed to thinking about literature and politics, he had no real concept of the price mechanism. He thought that profits must be extorted by power. For example, he assumed that capitalists would always deliberately suppress innovation to keep profits high. He believed that this had actually happened to a type of 'flexible glass' that had been mentioned in antiquity by the Roman writer Petronius, but was now irretrievably lost.

In fact, however, capitalists are slaveringly eager to innovate, to cut into each other's market share. Perhaps when Orwell was growing up, it was possible to argue hypothetically that the Soviet Union would innovate faster. But as it turned out, it was precisely at innovation that capitalism beat communism most decisively.

Because capitalists are always trying to stab each other in the back, free markets do not lead to monopolies. Essentially, monopolies can only exist when governments support them. For example, the media business in this country is relatively concentrated at least in part because of Canberra's restrictions against foreign ownership (and monopolies are quite often mirages – people just have not thought carefully enough about what constitutes the relevant market. For example, both advertisers and audiences in fact do have alternatives to newspapers – radio, television, eventually quite possibly the telephone system – throughout Australia.) The fact that Orwell did not understand markets leads to one of the most pointed, and indeed poignant, differences between Orwell's *Nineteen Eighty-Four* and Peter Huber's rewriting of it in *Orwell's Revenge.* In *Nineteen Eighty-Four*, the street markets run by the proles and technically illegal, are drab and depressing places. But in Huber's scenario, they are lively, bustling – indeed, they provide better goods and services than the party's official outlet. You get the impression that the proles have implicitly declared independence from the party state. It withers away, although not at all in the way Marx expected.

Again, we know from the collapse of communism that this is entirely realistic. In the Soviet bloc, the black market rapidly became the only effective way to get anything of value, and grey markets in the Soviet Union itself, towards the end. Some vast proportion of all produce sold came from the minute fraction of agricultural land that peasants were allowed to cultivate themselves.

As Huber points out in his book, it is the hijacked telescreen system itself that has really unleashed the elemental power of these private street markets. The proles are able to use it to trade goods. In economists' jargon, it makes possible the more efficient allocation of resources.

The poignant aspect of this is that Orwell did have some dim inkling of what street markets could mean. In one of his earlier novels, he provided a lyrical description of one (which Peter Huber promptly appropriated for his rewritten book). And in that novel, Orwell had his hero reflect on the scene as follows: 'whenever you see a street market you know that there is hope for England yet.'

That's a moment of true artistic insight – albeit unsupported (as sometimes happens with artists) with any rational or scientific follow-through. The freedom, the unforced exchange of the street market, its pragmatic acceptance of human self-interest and its transformation of self-interest into something mutually, peacefully beneficial – it does mean there is hope for England ... and, indeed, for all of us in the Western world.

It's not an accident that Napoleon called England a nation of shopkeepers. What Orwell and Napoleon together saw, however confused or critical they felt about it, was the extent to which markets, or what I referred to earlier and more grandly as the principles of classical liberalism, are fundamental to our civilisation.

And this is the broader conclusion to which I said I would return.

I said earlier that we suffer from a congerie of attitudes that cause us to be surprised by the idea that technology might be beneficial – and perhaps by the underlying principle that free markets are fundamental to our civilisation.

A part of that congerie is the eclipse into which the idea of markets passed for a considerable part of this century. For a variety of reasons, it was assumed by Left and Right alike, and indeed it is still too often assumed, that markets do not work properly and that governments have to step in. I'm not talking about communism here, or even socialism, but about all pervasive regulation and control.

And that assumption still underlies many of our Australian institutions – notably our labour market, the bone in Australia's throat, something which I know the Centre for Independent Studies has examined recently – with appropriate distaste.

When you rethink this assumption about markets, you see the world through different eyes. It wasn't just the Soviets who thought that street markets were the work of speculators and assorted anti-social elements. The entire establishment of Western development economists viewed them as trivial at best, unproductive middlemen at worst.

Well, at News Corporation we are enlightened. For example, in India we have discovered that tens of thousands of pirates have invested in reception dishes and are selling STAR programming to a few hundred, sometimes just a few score, households in their immediate neighbourhood.

Some cynics have said this will be fatal for our Asian television company, STAR. We disagree. Indeed, we look forward to a long partnership with these splendid entrepreneurs. They are pioneering the market – a market that Orwell himself, who worked in the BBC's Indian service, said was fatally flawed because it did not yet embrace the masses.

The case of India, by the way, illustrates another important point: although technology does not lead to tyranny, neither need it lead to chaos. The new markets it creates don't just make Northcliffes rich: they may also solve age-old political problems.

Indian leaders have long been desperately worried about disunity in their vast, teeming, multilingual country. This is something we can hardly understand in the English-speaking world, where we achieved total political stability so long ago. To try to achieve it in India, there has been an effort ever since independence to promote Hindi as the lingua franca, what in India is called the 'link language'. But the effort has failed. Until now. With the coming of the electronic mass media, Hindi is finally spreading, because everyone wants to watch the best television programming. And I suspect we will see this story repeated throughout the developing world, not least in China with Mandarin.

In which case it will not only be prosperity that we will catch in our networks, but also order – and, ultimately, peace.

And peace, remember, has been in short supply in the twentieth century. The optimism of Northcliffe's 1890s gave way to the catastrophe of the First World War. And the First World War looms over this entire century, really only ending with the fall of the Soviet Union. In its dark shadow we dreamed the Orwellian totalitarian nightmare.

In *Nineteen Eighty-Four* George Orwell was a pessimist. But he was also an optimist – as I've said, you can't expect artists to be consistent. Earlier, he had written a poem about a young volunteer militia he saw in the Spanish civil war:

> No power can disinherit
> No bomb that ever burst
> Shatters the crystal spirit

Ladies and gentlemen, in this century of bursting bombs, I like to think that we are doing our part, however humble and mundane to free that crystal spirit.

Vote of Thanks

Kenneth P. Baxter

Secretary, Victorian Department of Premier and Cabinet

Mr Chairman, Mr Murdoch, Dame Elisabeth, Mrs Bonython, distinguished guests, ladies and gentlemen. Having been preceded by a question from the ABC and one from *The Sydney Morning Herald*, I thought, Mr Murdoch, I should add the third lie, 'I'm here from the government and I'm here to help you.'

I thought it also appropriate tonight that you started with a reference to Lord Northcliffe and *The Daily Mail.* Because as my counterpart in the United Kingdom, Sir Humphrey Appleby, once observed to Jim Hacker when he was only a Minister, *The Daily Mail* is read by the wives of the people who run the country, which I thought was very foresighted of Lord Northcliffe back in the 1890s. But he didn't also foresee that *The Times* is read by the people who run the country; *The Daily Mirror* is read by the people who think they run the country; *The Guardian* is read by the people who think they ought to run the country (and perhaps that might be *The Sydney Morning Herald*); *The Financial Times* is read by the people who own the country; *The Daily Telegraph* is read by the people who still think that it is their country; and of course *The Sun* readers don't care who runs the country providing that she has big tits.

Tonight's speech was a rare one in that it displays a sense of vision, a pursuit of talent, a passion for technology and innovation, and something, with respect Sir, where I think we civil servants have been ahead of you for a long time – a desire for networking. We've managed to do without technology and stuffed things up generally very well right around the world!

But I can say, in traditional civil service fashion, that I am officially advised that my Premier's government would be pleased about the vigorous and very persuasive promotion of the role and dynamism of the free market. I've also got to say that it was very rewarding to have an extraordinary man of great ideas to have presented the 1994 John Bonython Lecture. It is all the more significant because visionary men of ideas leading international newspaper and media chains are few and far between. I doubt if we have any other Australians in that category, and long may he live. We should also have immense respect for his mother, who has clearly kept him on the straight and narrow and maintained his sense of innovation.

Tonight I'd like to pay a tribute to another great man in Australia, Greg Lindsay, and his organisation of ideas. Without Greg's energy and innovation, tonight would not have happened. Nor would it have happened without Anna Kasper and Kate Patterson who are here with us, and Amanda Wright in Sydney. The success of tonight is due in no small way to their efforts.

Mr Murdoch, no matter what some of us around this room may think of you or claim that they think of you, I hope that both you and the CIS and others who walk with you, will in fact 'free the crystal spirit', and we look forward to the peace of the next century.

